How to Draw
WILD ANIMALS

Barbara Soloff Levy

DOVER PUBLICATIONS, INC.
Mineola, New York

Note

With *How to Draw Wild Animals* as your guide, you won't have to fear venturing into the unknown territory of drawing a variety of beasts. Any armchair explorer will be able to recognize the creatures you create. From aardvark to yak, from badger to walrus, you'll find a multitude of four-footed animals from all parts of the world. In addition, a bat, a cobra, an ostrich, a peacock, and a penguin are included. You'll learn how to draw each creature by following four steps that use simple shapes to produce a good likeness. After you've drawn some of these 30 animals, you can use this easy method to draw other favorite animals.

Copyright

Copyright © 1999 by Barbara Soloff Levy
All rights reserved under Pan American and International Copyright Conventions.

Published in Canada by General Publishing Company, Ltd., 30 Lesmill Road, Don Mills, Toronto, Ontario.

Bibliographical Note

How to Draw Wild Animals is a new work, first published by Dover Publications, Inc., in 1999.

Library of Congress Cataloging-in-Publication Data

Soloff-Levy, Barbara.
 How to draw wild animals / Barbara Soloff Levy.
  p.   cm.
 ISBN 0-486-40821-3 (pbk.)
  1. Animals in art.   2. Drawing—Technique.   I. Title.
 NC780.S633   1999
 743.6—dc21
                                                                99-32164
                                                                CIP

Manufactured in the United States of America
Dover Publications, Inc., 31 East 2nd Street, Mineola, N.Y. 11501

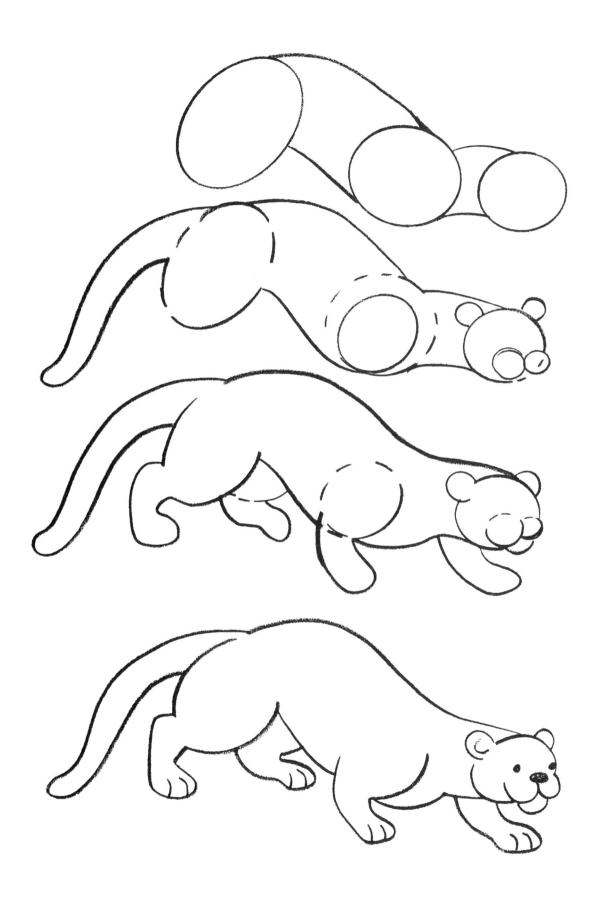

4   GORILLA

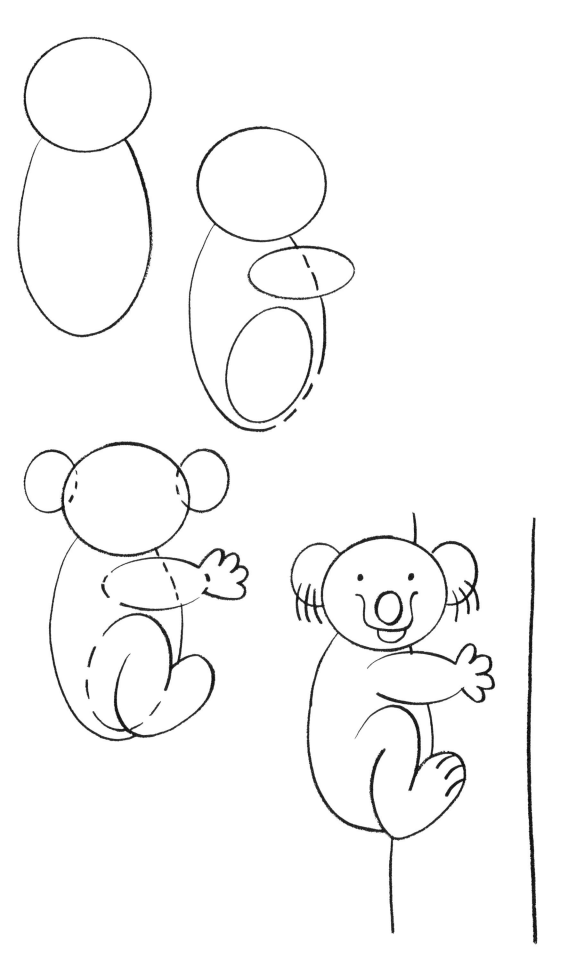

ORANGUTAN

PENGUIN   9

YAK

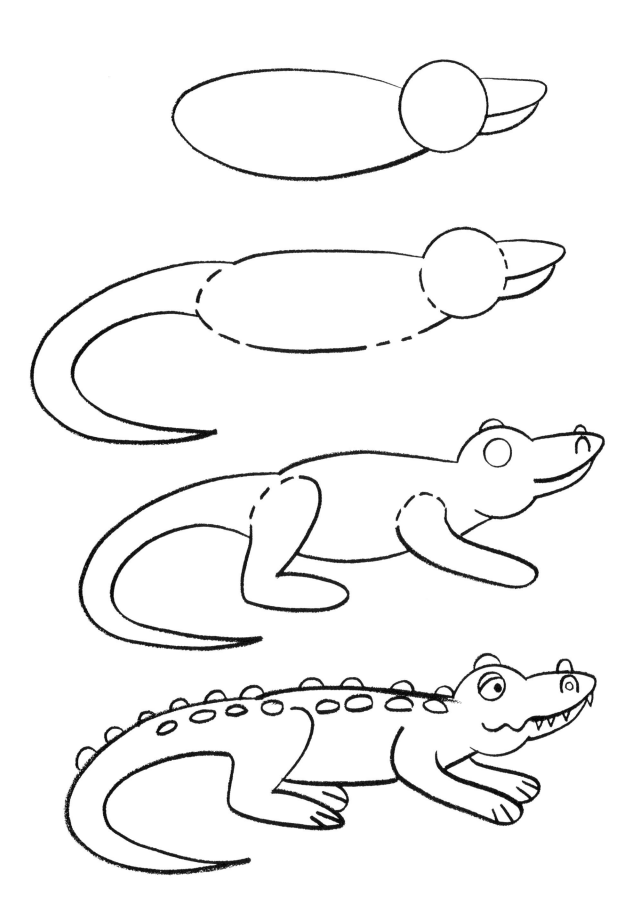

14   POLAR BEAR

WALRUS

LLAMA

　LION

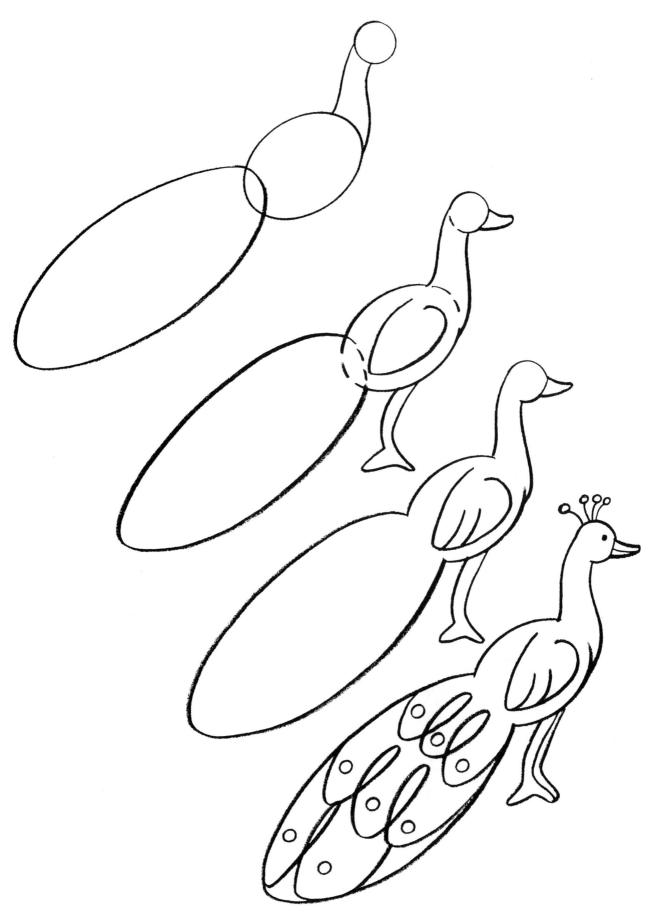

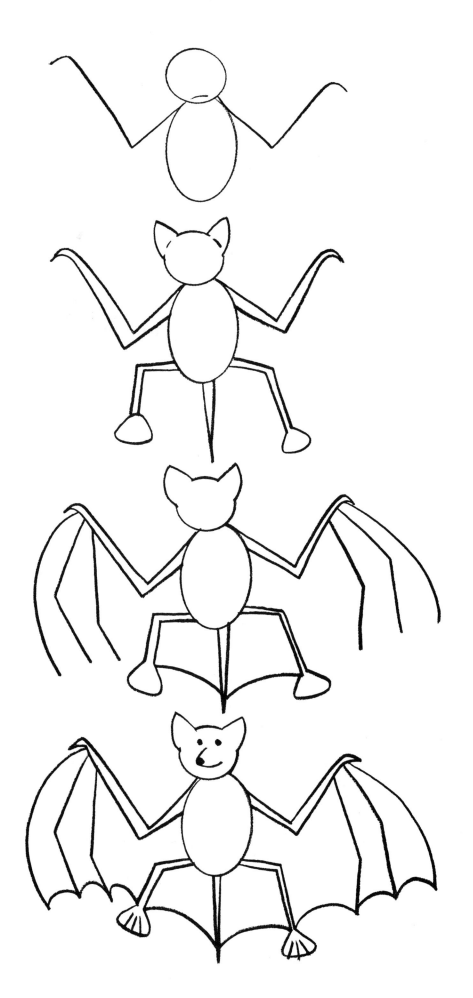

BAT

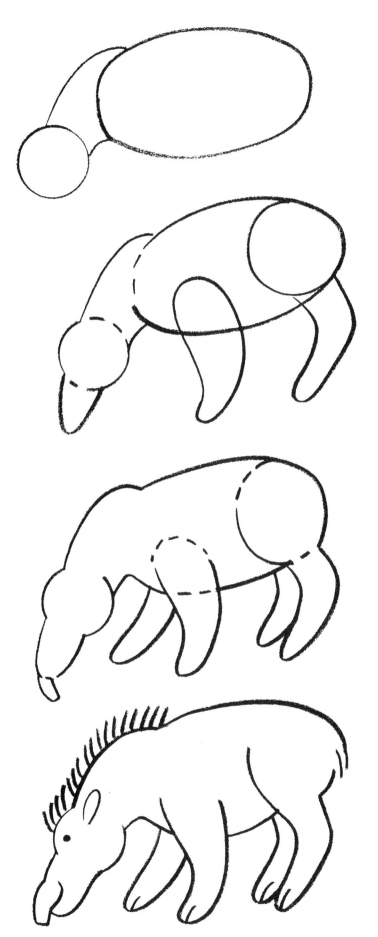

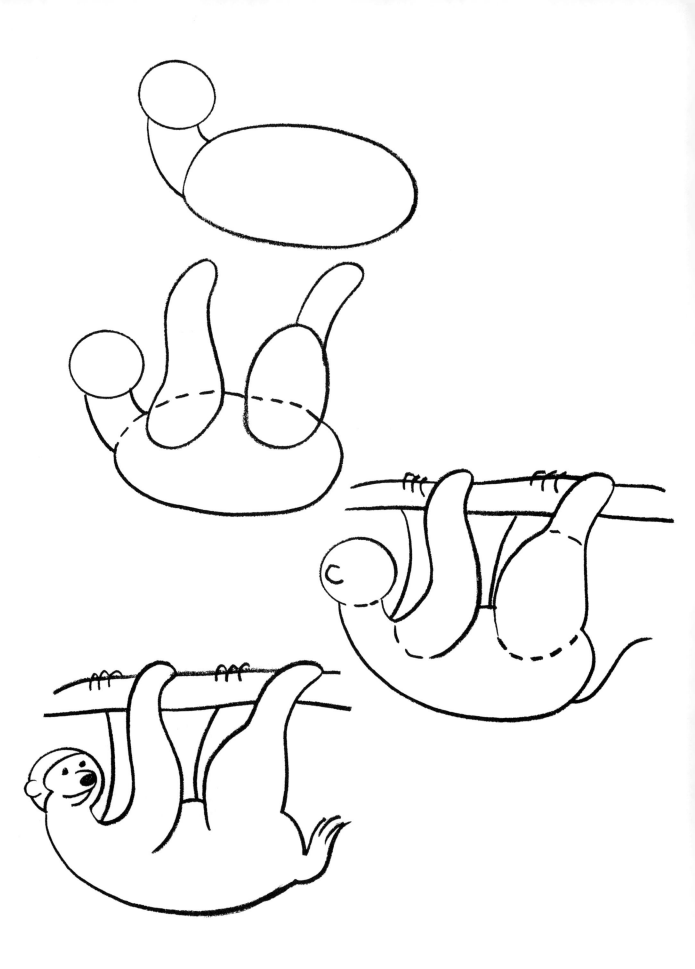

SLOTH